First Church of Worcester, Mass.

The History, Articles of Faith, Covenant and Standing Rules

of the First church in Worcester, Mass.

with a catalogue of its officers and members

First Church of Worcester, Mass.

The History, Articles of Faith, Covenant and Standing Rules of the First church in Worcester, Mass.
with a catalogue of its officers and members

ISBN/EAN: 9783337159405

Printed in Europe, USA, Canada, Australia, Japan

Cover: Foto ©Lupo / pixelio.de

More available books at **www.hansebooks.com**

THE HISTORY,

ARTICLES OF FAITH,

COVENANT,

AND

STANDING RULES,

OF

THE FIRST CHURCH

IN WORCESTER, MASS.

WITH A

Catalogue of its Officers and Members.

APRIL, 1, 1864.

WORCESTER:
ADAMS & BROWN, PRINTERS, 212 MAIN STREET.
(SUCCESSORS TO H. J. HOWLAND.)

CHURCH ORGANIZED IN THE YEAR 1716.

OFFICERS OF THE CHURCH, 1864.

PASTOR.

Rev. EDWARD ASHLEY WALKER,

DEACONS.

RICHARD BALL,
CALEB DANA,
SAMUEL W. KENT,
CHARLES A. LINCOLN.

CLERK.

CALEB DANA.

TREASURER.

RICHARD BALL.

HISTORY.

In the spring of 1674, a company of thirty persons commenced the first settlement in Worcester, but the breaking out of King Phillip's war in the following year led them to abandon the enterprise.

A second attempt at a settlement was made in 1684, and continued to progress for eighteen years until the commencement of Queen Anne's war in 1702, when the project was again abandoned. The third and first effectual settlement of the place, was commenced by Jonas Rice, who returned to the town, Oct. 21, 1713. He remained the sole inhabitant till the spring of 1715, when he was joined by his brother Gershom, who came, as he himself had done, from Marlborough.

The first settlers of Worcester began their enterprise under formal and written obligation to secure the services of a clergyman, erect a meeting-house, and maintain religious worship, at the earliest possible day. Until a minister could be obtained, the inhabitants were required to assemble on the Sabbath in social religious meetings. With this requisition they evinced every disposition to comply. The first meetings for devotional exercises were held in the house of Gershom Rice. This was probably in 1715 or 1716. In the year 1716, or in the early part of 1717, the First Church in Worcester was organized, and Daniel Heywood and Nathaniel Moore were chosen its Deacons. Soon afterwards, a small meeting-house was built near the spot where at present Green street forms a junction with Park and Franklin streets. This house was constructed of logs, and was erected in 1717.

In 1719, a second meeting-house was erected. It appears to have been considerably larger than the first, and better adapted to the purposes of religious worship. The site selected was on the common, near the spot where the present edifice stands. In the autumn of the same year, the REV. ANDREW GARDNER was ordained as the first pastor. He was a native of Brookline, Mass., and graduated at Harvard University in 1712. Mr. Gardner continued his ministry for the term of three years, and was dismissed by a mutual council on the 31st of October, 1722.

The pastoral office remained vacant until the 30th of October, 1725, when the REV. ISAAC BURR, the second pastor, was ordained. Mr. Burr was a native of Fairfield, Conn., and graduated at Yale College in 1717. Mr. Burr sustained his relation to the Church and Parish for a period of twenty years, and at his own request was dismissed by an ecclesiastical council, in March, 1745.

On the 22d of Sept. 1746, the following Covenant was adopted at a meeting of the Church convened for that purpose, and signed by fifty of its members, and attested by Rev. John Campbell of Oxford, and Rev. John Prentice of Lancaster:

COVENANT.

"We whose names are hereunto subscribed, being inhabitants of the town of Worcester, in New England, knowing that we are very prone to offend and provoke God, Most High, both in heart and life, through the prevalency of sin that dwelleth in us, and the manifold temptations from without us, for which we have great reason to be unfeignedly humble before him, from day to day, do, in the name of our Lord and Savior, Jesus Christ, with dependence upon the gracious assistance of his Holy Spirit, solemnly enter into covenant with God, and with one another, according to his holy direction, as follows ;

" First : That having chosen and taken the Lord Jehovah, Father, Son, and Holy Spirit, to be our God, we will fear him, cleave to him in love, and serve him in truth, with all our hearts, giving up ourselves to him to be his people, in all things to be at his direction and sovereign disposal, that we may have and hold communion with him, as members of Christ's mystical body, according to his revealed will, to our life's end.

" Secondly : We bind ourselves to bring up our children and servants, in the knowledge and fear of God, by his instructions, according to our best abilities ; and, in special, by orthodox catechisms, viz. the Assembly's at Westminster larger and shorter catechisms, that the true religion may be maintained in our families while we live ; yea, and among such as shall survive us, when we are dead and gone.

" Thirdly : We furthermore promise, to keep close to the truth of Christ, endeavoring with lively affections of it in our hearts, to defend it against all opposers thereof, as God shall call us at any time thereunto ; which, that we may do, we resolve to use the Holy Scriptures as our directory, whereby we may discern the mind and will of Christ, and not the new found inventions of men.

" Fourthly : We also engage ourselves, to have a careful inspection over our hearts, so as to endeavor, by virtue of the death of Christ, the mortification of our sinful passions, worldly frames, and disorderly affections, whereby we may be withdrawn from the living God.

" Fifthly : We furthermore oblige ourselves in the faith-

1*

ful improvement of all our abilities and opportunities, to worship God, according to the particular institutions of Christ for his church, under gospel administrations ; to give a reverent attention to the word of God ; to pray unto him ; to sing his praises ; and to hold communion with one another, in the use of both the sacraments of the New Testament, viz. Baptism and the Lord's Supper.

" Sixthly : We likewise promise, that we will peaceably submit ourselves, unto the holy discipline appointed by Christ in his church, for offenders, obeying, according to the will of God, them that rule over us in the Lord.

" Seventhly : We also bind ourselves, to walk in love one towards another, endeavoring our mutual edification, visiting, exhorting, comforting as occasion serveth, any brother or sister which offends ; not divulging private offences irregularly, but heedfully following the several precepts laid down by Christ for church discipline, in the xviii. of Matthew, 15, 16, 17 ; willingly forgiving all that manifest, unto the judgment of charity, that they truly repent of all their miscarriages.

" Now, the God of peace, which brought again from the dead our Lord and Savior Jesus Christ, the Great Shepherd of the sheep, through the blood of the everlasting covenant, make us all perfect in every good word and work, to do his will, working in us that which is well pleasing in his sight, through Jesus Christ, to whom be glory forever and ever. Amen.

The Rev. Thaddeus Maccarty of Boston, the third pastor, was installed, June 10, 1747, the pastor elect preaching the sermon from 1st Thes. ii. 13. Mr. Maccarty was minister of the town during the Revolutionary war. He was a graduate of Harvard College, of the class of 1739. He died " in peace, faith and hope," July 20, 1784, after a useful ministry of thirty-seven years. It was during the ministry of Mr. Maccarty that the present house of worship was erected. It was finished in 1763. Having undergone several modifications at different times, it has now stood more than one hundred years.

After an interval of some years, the REV. SAMUEL AUSTIN, of New Haven, a youthful soldier in the revolutionary war, and a graduate of Yale College, of the class of 1784. accepted an invitation to assume the pastoral charge, and was installed Sept. 30th, 1790. The Rev. Samuel Hopkins, of Hadley, his father-in-law, preached on the occasion.

Mr. Austin had been educated for the legal profession, but, having changed his course to theology, he became a pupil of the younger Dr. Edwards. At this period, the Church adopted a series of Articles of Faith, and also a new Covenant, both of which, with some verbal alterations, are still retained. It does not appear from the records extant, that the Church had adopted any Articles of Faith at any previous period of its history. In 1815, Rev. Dr. Austin was elected President of the University of Vermont, and accepted the appointment. He still, however, retained the nominal pastorship of the First Church in Worcester, in compliance with the express desire of the Church and Parish.

On the 9th of October, 1816, the REV. CHARLES A. GOODRICH, of Berlin, Conn., was ordained as colleague pastor of the Church, it being stipulated in the agreement that he was to be sole pastor upon the dismission of Dr. Austin, which latter event took place on the 23d of December, 1818, Mr. Austin's ministry having continued about thirty years. Mr. Goodrich, now the sole pastor of the Church and Parish, was at length dismissed, at his own request, Nov. 14th, 1820.

The Rev. Aretius B. Hull was the next minister.
He was ordained on the 22d of May, 1821. The Rev.
Nathaniel W. Taylor, D. D. of New Haven, delivered the
sermon. Mr. Hull was born at Woodbridge, Conn., Oct.
12, 1788. His parents were emigrants from England,
highly respectable in character. He graduated at Yale
College in 1807. Mr. Hull had been subject to the usual
infirmities of a feeble constitution from his youth. In
the spring of 1825, his physical debility became so serious
as to reduce him to the necessity of desisting from his ministerial work. He died on the 17th of May, 1826, in the
38th year of his age, and the 5th of his ministry in Worcester.

The next year, namely, in February, 1827, the Rev.
Rodney A. Miller received an invitation to become the
pastor of the First Church and Parish. Having communi-
cated his acceptance, he was ordained June 7, 1827. The
sermon was preached by the Rev. Warren Fay, D. D., of
Charlestown. Mr. Miller was descended from a puritan
family, who emigrated from Devonshire, England, and
settled near Hampton, on the east end of Long Island.
They subsequently removed to Troy, New York. Mr.
Miller graduated at Union College, in 1821, and pursued
the usual course of theological studies at the Princeton
Seminary, New Jersey. The Rev. Mr. Miller was dismissed from the pastoral care of the First Church in Worcester, by a mutual Council, April 12, 1844, after a long and
successful ministry in this place of almost seventeen years.
Accompanying the act of dismission on the part of the
council, was a formal testimony, of the most satisfactory
character, as to his moral worth and ministerial efficiency.

After a vacancy of nearly one year in the pastoral office,
the Rev. George Phillips Smith, of South Woburn
(now Winchester,) having received and accepted a call,

became the eight pastor of the church, and was installed March 19th, 1845. The sermon on this occasion was delivered by the Rev. Thomas Snell, D. D., of North Brookfield.

Mr. Smith was born in Salem, Mass., on the 11th of February, 1814, and was a graduate of Amherst College, of the class of 1835, and of Andover Theological Seminary, of the class of 1840.

The Rev. Mr. Smith died at Salem on the third day of September, 1852, in the thirty-ninth year of his age, and in the eighth of his ministry in Worcester. By his kind and affectionate spirit he endeared himself to the people of his charge and a large circle of friends, by whom his death was deeply lamented.

On the 13th day of December, 1852, the church and parish with great unanimity invited the REV. HORACE JAMES of Wrenthem, Mass., to become their pastor and minister. Mr. James accepted the invitation, and was installed on the 3d day of February, 1853, on which occasion the sermon was preached by the Rev. Edwards A. Park, D. D., of Andover.

Mr. James, is a native of Medford, Mass. He graduated at Yale College in 1840, and pursued a course of theological study at New Haven and Andover.

In October 1861, Mr. James having been appointed Chaplain of the 25th Regiment of Massachusetts Volunteers, tendered his resignation as Pastor and left with his regiment, in Gen. Burnside's expedition, for North Carolina. In 1863 he was appointed Superintendent of freedmen in the Department of N. C.

Mr. James' ministerial relation to this Church and Parish was dissolved, at his own request, by an ecclesiastical Council, Jan'y 8, 1863, with their testimony to his activity, fidelity, and success as a christian minister.

In June following, the Church and Parish, by their unan-
imous votes, in concurrence, extended an invitation to the
REV. EDWARD ASHLEY WALKER, of New Haven, Conn.
to become their Pastor and settle with them in the work
of the christain ministry.   Mr. Walker accepted the invitation, and was Installed July 2d, 1863.   The sermon on
the occasion, was preached by Rev. Willard Child, D. D.
of Castleton, Vt.

Mr. Walker was born at New Haven, Conn., Nov. 24,
1834, graduated at Yale College in the class of 1856,
pursued his professional studies at New Haven and at the
universities of Heidelberg and Berlin, Germany, and was
ordained at New Haven, June 5, 1861, Chaplain of the
1st Conn. Vol. Heavy Artillery.   After serving 15 months
he was compelled by sickness to resign his position in the
army.

On the 22d day of September, 1863, the Church and
Parish commemorated the hundreth anniversary of the
erection of their Meeting-house.   It appears by an entry
made upon the Church records by the Rev. Mr. Maccarty,
that the house "began to be erected June 21, 1763," and
that it was first used for religious purposes, "Dec. 8, 1763,"
on which occasion he preached a sermon from I Chr. xxix.
16, 17.   The day of the centennial commemoration was
selected as occurring at a more favorable season than that on
which the house was commenced, or dedicated.   An intro-
ductory address was made by the Hon. Ira M. Barton.
The historical discourse was delivered by Rev. Leonard
Bacon, D. D., of the First Church in New Haven, Conn.
All the services were of an interesting character, and highly
appreciated by a large and respectable audience.

FORM OF ADMISSION.

ADDRESS.

BELOVED FRIENDS; You have presented yourselves before God, and his people, and before the world, to make a public profession of your religious faith, and to take upon you everlasting obligations. We trust you have well considered the nature of this transaction, the most solemn and momentous in which a mortal can ever engage, and that you are prepared by divine grace to give yourselves away, a living sacrifice, holy and acceptable to God, through Jesus Christ.

Having been duly examined and propounded, and having assented in private to the articles of faith adopted by this church, you will now profess the same before these witnesses.

CONFESSION OF FAITH.

I. You believe that there is one only living and true God; a being, independent and eternal in his existence and glory; unchangeable in his purposes; possessed of infinite power, wisdom, justice, goodness and truth; and who is the Creator, Preserver, Benefactor, and righteous moral Governor of the universe.

II. You believe that the scriptures of the Old and New Testaments were given by inspiration of God, and are the only perfect rule of faith and practice.

III. You believe the scriptures teach that God exists in a manner incomprehensible to us, under a threefold distinction, as Father, Son, and Holy Ghost; and that these three, possessing equal perfections, are one God,

IV.   You believe that the only true standard of holiness is the divine law, that its trangression is sin, and its penalty the second death; and that all men, as free moral agents, are under solemn obligation perfectly to obey the law of God.

V.   You believe that our first parents were created holy; that they fell from their happy state by transgressing the divine command; and that, in consequence of their apostasy, the heart of man until it is renewed by the Holy Spirit, is destitute of holiness and alienated from God.

VI.   You believe that those who are renewed by the Spirit of God, were ordained from the foundation of the world, by an election purely of grace, unto everlasting life; and that they will be kept by the power of God, through faith, unto final salvation.

VII.   You believe that the only Redeemer of mankind is the Lord Jesus Christ, who became incarnate that he might offer an effectual sacrifice for sin by the death of the cross; that by this sacrifice he became the propitiation for the sins of men, and that all who are saved will be entirely indebted to the grace of God, through the atonement.

VIII.   You believe that the Gospel is freely and sincerely offered to all, and that all are under obligation immediately to embrace it; and that repentance and faith in the Lord Jesus Christ, are indispensable to salvation.

IX.   You believe that there will be a resurrection of the dead and a day of general judgment, when the rightous will be received to the perfect and endless enjoyment of God in heaven, and the wicked will be sentenced to everlasting punishment.

X.   You believe that the sacraments of the church are Baptism and the Lord's Supper.   That visible believers only, who receive the truth in the love of it, and maintain a deportment becoming the gospel, have a right to partake of the Lord's Supper ; and that they, with their households, are the only proper subjects of Christian Baptism.

To this summary of Christian doctrine you cordially assent ?

[*Here the ordinance of Baptism is administered to those who have not been baptized. And those who were baptized in infancy are reminded that they do now voluntarily accept, as a token of their own personal faith, and as the seal of a believer's hope, the rite which was originally a pledge of God's faithfulness to their pious parents, on their behalf.*]

You will now enter into Covenant with God, and with this Church.

COVENANT.

You do now, in the presence of God, angels and men, solemnly take the Lord Jehovah, Father, Son, and Holy Ghost, to be your God, the object of your supreme love, and your portion. You receive, trust in, and desire to obey, the Lord Jesus Christ as your only Redeemer. You choose the Holy Spirit as your Sanctifier. You give up yourselves and all that you have to God, to be his ; desiring, above all things, to be instruments of his glory in that way which he shall see best. And promising, through the help of divine grace, without which you can do nothing, that you will deny ungodliness and worldly lusts, and that you will live soberly, righteously and godly, even unto death. You cordially join yourselves to this Church,

2

as a true church of our Lord Jesus Christ, and engage to be subject to its discipline, so far as it is conformable to the rules Christ has given in the Gospel; and that you will walk with the members thereof, in all holy love, watchfulness and purity.

This you (severally) promise and engage?

[*Here the church will rise.*]

And now do we, the members of this church, in consequence of these your professions and promises, affectionately receive you to our communion; and in the name of Christ declare you entitled to all its visible privileges. We welcome you to a fellowship with us in the blessings of the gospel; severally engaging, on our part, to love you as Christians, to watch over you, to pray for you, and seek your edification so long as you shall continue among us. Should you have occasion to remove, it will be your duty to seek, and ours to grant, a recommendation to another church; for hereafter you can never withdraw from the watch and communion of the saints, without a breach of Covenant.

And now, Beloved in the Lord, let it be impressed on your minds that you have entered into solemn relations, which you can never renounce, and from which you can never escape. Hereafter, the eyes of the world will be upon you. If you walk worthily, you will bring strength and gladness to our Zion; but if otherwise, you will be to us a grief and a reproach. Wherever you go, these vows will be upon you. They will follow you to the bar of God; and, in whatever world you may be fixed, they will abide upon you forever.

To Him, then, who is able to keep us from falling, and present us faultless before his throne with exceeding joy, we commend the keeping of our precious interests. May the Lord ever guide and preserve us, causing us to become more and more conformed to the example of our divine Master, till we come at last to the perfection of holiness, in the kingdom of his glory. Amen.

STANDING RULES.

I. The Annual Meeting of this Church shall be held on the Wednesday next preceding the first Sabbath in January, when the following officers shall be chosen, viz : A clerk and a Treasurer, who shall be chosen by ballot, a Committee of two to audit accounts, a Committee of four, who with the Pastor and Deacons shall constitute a Standing Committee.

II. It shall be the duty of the Clerk to keep the Records, forward all letters of dismission and recommendation of members, and report in writing, at the annual meeting of the church, a corrected catalogue of the members, with the number and names of all persons received, dismissed, excommunicated, or deceased, during the year.

III. It shall be the duty of the Treasurer to take charge of all money belonging to the Church and received at benevolent contributions, pay all bills and appropriations as voted by the church, except as specified in Rule XI; and render his account of all receipts and expenditures, properly vouched, at the annual meeting.

IV. It shall be the duty of the Standing Committee to report in writing at the annual meeting, the spiritual condition of the church during the year; to present a list of the non-resident members, giving their residence and standing; to keep a general oversight of all such members, holding correspondence with them when necessary; to conduct the examination of candidates for admission to the church; and to perform such other duty as the church may impose upon them.

V. Candidates for admission to this church by profession of faith, shall in ordinary cases be examined at a meeting of the church regularly called, and all questions touching their application shall be decided by vote of the church. They shall stand propounded at least two weeks, and no objection being presented, shall be received previously to the celebration of the Lord's Supper on a communion day.

VI. Candidates for admission by recommendation from other churches, may make application to either of the officers of the church, and present their letters. Notice of such application shall be given before the church, when assembled for the communion service, and the request shall be finally acted upon at a subsequent meeting of the church after an interval of not less time than two weeks.

VII. The Lord's Supper shall be celebrated on the first Sabbaths in January, March, May, July, September and November: and the Preparatory Lecture shall be on Friday of the week next preceding.

VIII. A meeting of the church for business and devotional exercises shall be held once in two months, viz: on the Friday next preceding the first Sabbaths in February, April, June, August, October and December. Church business may also be transacted at the stated meeting on Wednesday evening.

IX. Members who remove to other places, or worship and commune with other churches, are expected to procure letters of dismission and recommendation from this church within one year from the time of leaving us, unless they shall give reasons for their delay, satisfactory to the Standing Committee. Appended to every letter of dismission is a blank certificate, to be filled out and returned to us after the person shall have united with another church. No member shall be considered as discharged, until this certificate, properly filled out, has been returned to the clerk. Application for letters of dismission shall in every case, be made in writing.

X. The Standing Committee of this church, besides forming an acquaintance with all candidates for membership, are expected to converse with members of sister churches residing among and communing with us, and to invite them, if in regular church standing, to transfer their relation and unite with us, within a year after taking up their residence with us.

XI. It shall be the duty of the Deacons to visit the poor and infirm members of the Church, to distribute among them money contributed for this object, and, in the absence of the Pastor, to preside at all the business meetings and to provide for the conduct of other occasional meetings of the church.

XII. Any member of this church having cause of complaint against another, in cases of personal offence, should immediately seek to have it removed in a christian manner, the directions given in Matt. 18 : 15, 16, 17, being his guide ; and whenever a charge is brought before the church, it shall be in writing, and a copy of it be furnished to the offending member.

XIII. The Church shall designate at each Annual meeting such objects of benevolence as they deem worthy to be supported by public contributions during the year, with the time and manner of taking them up. And the Pastor of the church, or in his absence the Standing Committee, shall see that they are duly presented to the Congregation. Other charities may be occasionally presented at the discretion of the Pastor and the Standing Committee.

XIV. These rules may be altered or amended at any regular business meeting of the church, by a majority of those that vote, notice of said alteration or amendment having been given at a previous meeting.

The following Resolutions were unanimously adopted by the church, on the 30th Nov., 1849.

Resolved: That it is the duty of church members, as a body and as indviduals, to sustain a preached gospel by communicating of their substance in proportion as God has given them the ability.

Resloved: That neglecting to do our just proportion in sustaining the gospel is immoral in its tendency, pernicious in its effect, and deserves the rebuke of the church.

Resolved: That it is the duty of church members to unite with the parish, that they may assume legal responsibilities, and exercise civil privileges.

OFFICERS OF THE CHURCH,

FROM ITS ORGANIZATION.

PASTORS.

Rev. ANDREW GARDNER,
Ordained Autumn of 1719; Dismissed Oct. 31, 1722.

Rev. ISAAC BURR,
Ordained Oct. 13, 1725; Dismissed March, 1745.

Rev. THADDEUS MACCARTY,
Installed June 10, 1747. Died July 20, 1784.

Rev. SAMUEL AUSTIN, D. D.,
Installed Sept. 30, 1790; Dismissed Dec. 23, 1818.

Rev. CHARLES A. GOODRICH,
Ordained Oct. 9, 1816; Dismissed Nov. 14, 1820.

Rev. ARETIUS B. HULL,
Ordained May 22, 1821; Died May 17, 1826.

Rev. RODNEY A. MILLER,
Ordained June 7, 1827; Dismissed April 12, 1844.

Rev. GEORGE P. SMITH,
Installed March 19, 1845; Died Sept. 3, 1852.

Rev. HORACE JAMES,
Installed Feb. 3, 1853; Dismissed Jan. 8, 1863.

Rev. EDWARD ASHLEY WALKER,
Installed July 2, 1863.

DEACONS.

	Elected.	Died.	Aged.
Daniel Heywood,	1716,	April 12, 1773,	79
Nathaniel Moore,	"	Nov. 25, 1761,	84
Jonas Rice,	Jan. 14, 1748,	Sept. 22, 1753,	84
Thomas Wheeler,	" " "	Jan. 9, 1769,	74
Jacob Chamberlain,	Dec. 16, 1751,	March 17, 1790,	71
Samuel Miller,	" " "	Sept. 9, 1759,	81
Nathan Perry,	Nov. 5, 1783,	Feb. 14, 1806,	88
Thomas Wheeler,	" " "	Jan. 12, 1795,	66
John Chamberlain,	Nov. 15, 1791,	May 31, 1813,	68
Leonard Worcester,	Oct. 19, 1797,	May 28, 1846,	79
David Richards,	Nov. 23, 1801,	Jan. 29, 1829,	78
Moses Perry,	June 18, 1807,	March 12, 1842,	80
John Nelson,	April 16, 1812,	Jan. 14, 1834,	72
Lewis Chapin,	Jan. 30, 1833,	Resigned 1843.	
Moses Brigham,	" " "	Resigned 1837.	
Nathaniel Brooks,	Aug. 5, 1836,	Nov. 3, 1850,	53
Nahum Nixon,	" " "	Aug. 27, 1850,	62
John Bixby,	Sept. 30, 1836,	July 14, 1853.	81
Richard Ball,	Sept. 17, 1845,		
Allen Harris,	Oct. 1, 1845,	Feb. 3, 1864,	73, 9m
Jonas M. Miles,	" " "	Resigned 1859.	
Caleb Dana,	April 4, 1851.		
Samuel W. Kent,	Jan. 2, 1861.		
Charles A Lincoln,	Feb. 1, 1861.		

CATALOGUE.
Present Members of the Church,
April 1, 1864.

(In the following Catalogue, the numbers prefixed to the names, indicate the year of uniting with this Church.

The letters P. and L. show whether the person united by Profession of Faith or by Letter of Recommendation from another Church.

Non-resident members are designated by the letters *n. r.*

The names of members who are now absent in the army against the rebellion are designated by a *

Names enclosed in a brace, are husband and wife.

W. is used as an abreviation for wife, and wid. for widow.)

1858. Abbott, Ebenezer E., }		L.
1858. Abbott, Augusta, }		P.
1858. Abbott, Frederick E.,		P.
1846. Adams, Lucy Jane, w. of Henry C.,		P.
1850. Adams, Fanny A., w. of John,		L.
1845. Ainsworth, Mary N., wid. of Nathan,		L.
1855. Ainsworth, Mary Jane,		P.
1857. Ainsworth, Henry L., }		P.
1857. Ainsworth, Mary C., }		L.
1863. Ainsworth, Laura A.,		L.
1831. Albro, Isaac, }		P.
1848. Albro, Harriet N., }		L.
1861. Albro, Harriet M.,		P.
1847. Allis, Phebe,		L.
1847. Allis, Nancy,		L.
1847. Allis, Experience W.,		L.
1854. Alton, James E., }	*n r.*	L.
1854. Alton, Lura J., }	*n. r.*	L.
1847. Andrews, John D., }	*n. r.*	P.
1850. Andrews, Rosalia L., }	*n. r.*	P.
1860. Ayers, Warren, }		L.
1860. Ayers, Rachel S., }		L.

1860.	Ayers, Anna E.,	L.
1861.	Ayers, Martha D.,	P.
1852.	Bacon, Catharine B., wid. of Samuel, *n. r.*	L.
1847.	Bailey, George, }	L.
1847.	Bailey, Clarissa E , }	L.
1858.	Bailey, Caroline M.,	P.
1846.	Baker, Asa, }	L.
1846.	Baker, Lucy, }	L.
1837.	Baker, Lucy E.,	P.
1852.	Baker, Nancy,	P.
1863.	Baldwin Elizabeth D., wid. of Nathan,	L.
1831.	Ball, Richard, }	P.
1831.	Ball, Sarah M., }	P.
1849.	Ball, Anna W.,	P.
1838.	Ballard, Eliza Jane, w. of C. H.,	P.
1858.	Bancroft, Sarah S.,	P.
1859.	Bancroft, James H., }	L.
1859.	Bancroft, N. Rebecca, }	L.
1854.	Barber, Isaac, }	L.
1854	Barber, Lucy Ann, }	L.
1863.	Barber, Ellen O.,	P.
1836.	Barber, Mary C.,	P.
1858.	Barber, Ruth E.,	P.
1827.	Barber, Hannah, w. of Silas,	P.
1855.	Barber, Josiah, }	P.
1853.	Barber, Maria B., }	L.
1852.	*Barbour, Isaac R., Jr.,	P.
1850.	Barry, Harriet G., w. of R. W.,	P.
1837.	Bartlett, Ephraim W.,	L.
1840.	Barton, Elbridge, *n. r.*	P.
1845.	Barton, Maria W., w of Ira M , (1835, L)	L.
1855.	*Barton, George Edward,	P.
1858.	Barton, Mary H., w. of J. H.,	P.
1858.	Bellows, Horace,	P.
1854.	Bennett, Frances E., w. of William M.,	L.

1856. Bernard, Eliza H., wid. of David,		L.
1831. Bigelow, Eliza, w. of Walter R.,		P.
1853. Bigelow, Louisa E., w. of H. W.,		L.
1855. Bigelow, Amos E., }		L.
1860. Bigelow, Mary P., }		L.
1844. Billing, Clarissa, wid. of Aaron,		L.
1851. Biscoe, Selinda, wid. of Alden,		L.
1842. Blair, Elizabeth, wid. of Charles,		P.
1854. Blair, Robert Horace, }	n. r.	P.
1853. Blair, Lucy M., }	n. r.	P.
1831. Bliss, Sarah H., w. of Harrison,		P.
1858. Bliss, Harriette B., wid. of John H.,	n. r.	P.
1858. Blood, Francis, }		P.
1859. Blood, Julia Louisa, }		P.
1855. Blood, Maria W., w. of Otis H.,		L.
1854. Boyden, Martha, wid. of David,		L.
1857. Boyden, Joseph B., }		L.
1857. Boyden, Octavia F., }		L.
1858. Boyden, Hannah, M , w. of John,		L.
1856. Boynton, Cordelia A., w. of E. N.,		P.
1858. Bradley, Osgood, }		P.
1858. Bradley, Sarah Jane M. }		P.
1863. Brewster, Lucy, wid. of William A.,		L.
1857. Brigham, Mary, wid. of Hosea,	n. r.	L.
1842. Brigham, Leonard, }		P.
1846. Brigham, Susan H., }		L.
1827. Brooks, Mary, wid. of Dea. Nathaniel,		P.
1842. Brooks, Charles E.,		P.
1838. Brown, Sarah, wid. of Larned,		P.
1860. Buel, Elizabeth, w. of Samuel K.,		L.
1849. Budd, John,	n. r.	P.
1849. Bugbee, Lyman, }		L.
1849. Bugbee, Mary T., }		L.
1318. Burbank, Betsey, w. of Isaac,	n. r.	P.
1817. Burnett, Cynthia, wid. of Luther,		P.

1842. Burr, Pedy L.,   P.
1852. Buttrick, Albert C.,   }   P.
1858. Buttrick, Elizabeth S,   }   L.

1859. Campbell, Lucy, w. of Daniel,   L.
1863. Capron, Edmund P.,   }   L.
1863. Capron, Anna E.,   }   L.
1858. Carew, Mary A.,   P.
1846. Carpenter, Eph'm W.,   }   *n. r.*   L.
1855. Carpenter, Sarah A.,   }   *n. r.*   P.
1863. Carpenter, Lucy M., w. of P. H.,   L.
1858. Carter, Abigail,   L.
1858. Carter, Milton T.,   }   P.
1857. Carter, Susan H.,   }   L.
1828. Chadwick, Mary, wid. of Daniel,   P.
1827. Chamberlin, Arathusa, wid. of Harmon,   P.
1857. Chamberlin, Arathusa H.,   P.
1828. Chamberlain, Hannah B., wid. of Thomas,   P.
1853. Chamberlain, Dora C.,   P.
1858. Chamberlain, Eph'm F.,   }   L.
1842. Chamberlain, Maria A,   }   P.
1846. Champney, Francis C.,   *n. r.*   L.
1858. Chapman, Lucy A., w. of Wm. R.,   P.
1858. *Chase, Wm. M.,   *n. r.*   P.
1858. Childs, Jane Elizabeth, w. of Norman,   L.
1850. Chollar, John,   }   L.
1850. Chollar, Elizabeth L.,   }   L.
1858. Clapp, Caroline K., wid. of Levi,   L.
1850. Clapp, Simeon,   }   L.
1850. Clapp, Lucy Ann,   }   L.
1838. Clark, Wm. L,   }   P.
1839. Clark, Lucretia,   }   L.
1852. Clark, John,   }   L.
1852. Clark, Sarah R.,   }   L.

1858. Clark, Anna R.,	P.
1855. Clark, Lucy P.,	L.
1858. Clark, Susan S.,	P.
1838. Clement, Sarah W.,	P.
1858. Clement, Caroline R.,	P.
1851. Clifford, Lorinda H., w. of Warner,	L.
1846. Cobb, Albert G.,	L.
1858. Cobb, Catharine S.,	P.
1864. Cobb, Harriet S.,	P.
1864. Cobb, E. Flora,	P.
1831. Cobleigh, Sophia, w. of Henry, *n. r.*	P.
1863. Coes, Abbie Winch, w. of Aury G.,	L.
1849. Conant, Martha H. P., w. of Otis,	L.
1833. Cook, Sumner,	L.
1831. Cook, Sophia,	P.
1858. Cook, John R.,	P.
1842. Curby, Elizabeth, *n. r.*	P.
1827. Curby, Polly,	P.
1858. Currier, Augustus N.,	P.
1858. Currier, Margaretta P.,	L.
1813. Curtis, Nancy, wid. of John,	P.
1837. Curtis, Geo. T. S., *n. r.*	P.
1849. Curtis, Harriet F., *n. r.*	L.
1836. Curtis, Sarah Ann,	P.
1842. Curtis, Joseph,	P.
1842. Curtis, Eunice,	P.
1858. Curtis, Caroline E.,	P.
1833. Curtis, Hannah S., wid. of Benj. F.,	L.
1837. Curtis, Lydia, *n. r.*	P.
1827. Cutting, Lewis, *n. r.*	P.
1857. Cutting, Sarah, wid. of Frederic,	L.
1849. Dana, Caleb,	L.
1849. Dana, Laurenda,	L.

3

1849. Dana, Mary L.,		L.
1839. Dana, Ebenezer,		L.
1845. Davis, Selina E., w. of Samuel,		L.
1854. Day, Eveline E. w. of Samuel,		L.
1842. Deland, Hester C.,	n. r.	P.
1850. Dickinson, Mary L., w. of William,		P.
1861. Dickson, Ellen A., w. of Joseph E.,	n. r.	P.
1858. Draper, Cornelia M.,		P.
1863. Drury, Lyman, }		L.
1863. Drury, Martha P., }		L.
1836. Duncan, Eliza,		P.
1861. Eames, Edwin A.,		L.
1864. Eames, Alfred M.,		P-
1858. Earle, Emma E., w. of Clark,		P.
1835. Eaton, Sally F., wid. of Thomas B.,		L.
1853. Eaton, A. J., }		L.
1853. Eaton, Delight, }		L.
1858. Eaton, Thomas,		L.
1858. Eaton, L. Adelia,		L.
1854. Eaton, Thomas S., }		P.
1863. Eaton, Martha M., }		L.
1854. Eddy, Samuel, Jr., }		L.
1861. Eddy Clara H., }		P.
1858. Eddy, Henry W., }		L.
1858. Eddy, Julia A., }		L.
1858. Eddy, Albert M.,		P.
1828. Elder, Dolly W., w. of Nath'l,		P.
1847. Elder, James,		L.
1858. Eldredge, Julius A., }	n. r.	P.
1858. Eldredge, Catharine, }	n. r.	P.
1852. Elliott, Gustavus, }		L.
1855. Elliott, Mary S. }		L.
1858. Elliott, Helena G.,		P.
1858. Ellis, Harriet H., w. of Nathan B.		P.

1845. Estabrook, James, }		L.
1845. Estabrook, Almira R. }		L.
1850. Estabrook, Rebecca, wid. of Stillman,	*n. r.*	L.
1861. Esten, Daniel S., }		L.
1861. Esten, Lorania H. }		L.
1852. Estey, Emily H., w. of James F.,	*n. r.*	L.
1863. Fairbanks, Joanna E., w. of Lewis T.,		L.
1842. Fairbanks, Cornelius W.,	*n. r.*	P.
1846. Farnum, Caroline,		L.
1858. Farnum, Lois M., w. of Joseph S ,		L.
1846. Fawcett, Jonathan, }		L.
1846. Fawcett, Asenath, }		L.
1853. Fay, John R.,		L.
1853. Fay, Emily E.,		L.
1853. Fay, Frederic E.,		L.
1863. Fay, Hamilton B., }		L.
1863. Fay, Hannah F., }		L.
1847. Fisher, Waterman A., }		L.
1847. Fisher, Louisa B., }		L.
1863. Fisher, Erastus, }		L.
1863. Fisher, Mary F., }		L.
1859. Fiske, Mary, wid. of Bezaleel,		L.
1859. Fiske, Matilda H., w. of Walter B.,	*n. r.*	P.
1858. Fitch, Dana H., }		P.
1858. Fitch, Melinda W., }		L.
1859. Fitch, Sarah C.,		P.
1854. Fitts, Benaiah, }		L.
1858. Fitts, Abby A., }		P.
1808. Flagg, Cynthia, wid. of Jonathan,		P.
1842. Flagg, Jarvis,	*n. r.*	P.
1859. Flagg, Waldo, }		P.
1859. Flagg, Mary A., }		P.
1859. Flagg, Caroline A., w. of Jos. W.,		L.
1854. Fletcher, Eliza, wid. of Joseph,		L.

1828. Foster, Elizabeth, wid. of Samuel,		P.
1860. Foster, Lucy H. wid. of Charles O.,		L.
1817. Fuller, Joseph D., ⎱	*n. r.*	L.
1848. Fuller, Caroline W., ⎰	*n. r.*	P.
1862. *Fuller, Warren A.,		L.
1860. Gardner, Elizabeth J.,		L.
1846. Gates, Ann,		L.
1842. Gates, Leonard, ⎱		P.
1842. Gates, Mary Jane, ⎰		P.
1857. Gates, Simon D.,		P.
1842. *Gates, Jaalam,		P.
1858. Gates, Ellen E.,		P.
1864. Gifford, Maria E., w. of Albert W.,		L.
1861. George, Elizabeth J., w. of George H.,		P.
1853. Gilbert, Mary, wid. of Charles,	*n. r.*	L.
1858. Gilbert, Charles W., ⎱		P.
1857. Gilbert, Calista B., ⎰		P.
1858. Gilbert, Achsah W.,		P.
1860. Gilman, Elizabeth C., wid. of Dr.,		L.
1856. Gleason, Lora,		L.
1842. Gleason, Sarah, wid. of John,	*n. r.*	P.
1858. Goddard, Sophia S.,		P.
1859. Goddard, Rebecca N.,		P.
1860. Goldard, D. B , ⎱ (L. 1851.)		L.
1860. Goddard, Sarah K , ⎰ (L. 1851)		L.
1863. Goddard, Sarah E ,		P.
1862. Goddard, Emmons A., ⎱		L.
1862. Goddard, Mary G., ⎰		L.
1858. Goodell, Eliza J. B., w. of John M ,		L.
1851. Goodman, Sarah, wid. of Eldad,		L.
1851. Goodman, Sarah B.,		L.
1854. Goodman, Caroline,		L.
1858. Goss, Emily A., w. of Brigham,		P.
1815. Gould, Hannah J., wid. of Ira M.,		L.

1801.	Greenleaf, Mary, wid. of Daniel,		P.
1831.	Greenleaf, Dolly Ann,		P.
1832.	Greenleaf, William, }		L.
1832.	Greenleaf, Myra J.,		L.
1858.	Grimshawe, Henry, }		P.
1856.	Grimshawe, Martha M.,		L.
1858.	Grimshawe, Julia Anna,		P.
1846.	Grout, William G., }		P.
1842.	Grout, Hannah C.,		P.
1858.	Grout, Emeline Carter, w. of Jacob B.,	n. r.	L.
1858.	Hall, Fannie E., w. of Alvin E.,	n. r.	P.
1852.	Hammond, Elijah, }		P.
1848.	Hammond, Caroline M.,		L.
1863.	Hammond, Lucy H , wid. of Edwin O.,		L.
1857.	Hanson, Charles H.,		L.
1847.	Harbach, Palmer, }		L.
1847.	Harbach, Abigail R.,		L.
1847.	Harding, Mary W., w. of Lorenzo,		P.
1849.	Harrington, Stephen, }		L.
1849.	Harrington, Sarah B.,		L.
1864.	Harrington, Lewis W.,		P.
1864.	Harrington, William A.,		P.
1843.	Harris, Almira, wid. of Allen,		L.
1850.	Hatch, Benjamin F.,		L.
1855.	Hawes, Clara N., w. Artemas,		P.
1831.	Hayden, Asa, }		P.
1854	Hayden, Emily G.,		L.
1848.	Hazeltine, Abigail R., wid. of Pardon,		L.
1857.	Hazeltine, Harriet S.,		P.
1864.	Hazeltine, Charles B. R.,		P.
1842.	Heard, Nathan,	n. r.	P.
1827.	Heywood, Henry,		P.
1842.	Heywood, Mary G., w. of W. H.,		P.
1858.	Hildreth, Matildia C., w. of Samuel E.,		P.

1849. Hill, Mary Ann S., w. of J. Q.,		P.
1858. Hill, Susan A., w. of Cornelius H.,		P.
1854. Hobbs, George 2d,		L.
1854. Hobbs, Louisa S.,		L.
1858. Holbrook, William D.,		P.
1858. Holbrook, Charlotte E.,		P.
1860. Holbrook, E. Anna,		L.
1863. Holden, Alfred,		L.
1863. Holden, Lucy M.,		I.
1858. Hool, Frances E. N.,		P.
1838. Houghton, Mirandia, wid. of Geo. W.,	n. r.	P.
1861. Houghton, Chas. S.,		P.
1859. Houghton, Mary,		L.
1842. Howe, Leonard,	n. r.	P.
1842. Howe, Nancy,	n. r.	P.
1861. Howe, Archelaus M ,		L.
1861. Howe, Hannah Janette,		L.
1824. Howe, Sarah H., wid. of William,		P.
1857. Howes, Arlette,	n. r.	L.
1858. Hoyle, Sarah L., w. of Wm.,		P.
1858. Hubbard, Cyrus K.,		L.
1858. Hubbard, Mary Elizabeth,		L.
1861. Hubbard, Henry B.,		L.
1861. Hubbard, Abby W.,		L.
1855. Hunt, Ann Maria,	n r.	P.
1854. Hutchinson, Mary Ann,		L.
1850. Jacobs, William H.,		L.
1850. Jacobs, Martha P.,		L.
1854. *James, Rev. Horace,		L.
1854. James, Helen,		L.
1838. Jaques, Susan,		P.
1861. Johnson, Elizabeth J., w. of Alex. H.,		L .
1817. Jones, John,		P.
1858. Joslin, Isaac Robinson,		L.
1850. Joslin, Laurinda B.		P.

1850. Kendall, Maria, w. of Smith,		P.
1848. Kendall, Dolly M.,		P.
1853. Kendall, Mary T., w. of John,		L.
1857. Kendall, Francis, }		L.
1857. Kendall, Mary E. }		L.
1854. Kent, Samuel W., }		L.
1854. Kent, Clara W., }		L.
1858. Kent, Ezra, }		L.
1858. Kent, Abigail B., }		L.
1858. Kimball, Juliette W.,		P.
1858. Kingman, Lydia A., w. of Davis,	n. r.	P.
1855. Klute, Henry,	n r.	P.
1842. Knapp, Louisa J., w. of Henry,	n. r.	P.
1857. Knapp, Lucinda, w. of Gilbert C.,	n. r.	L.
1848. Knight, Franklin H., }		L.
1848. Knight, Sarah E., }		L.
1863. Knight, Edna J.,		P.
1858. Knight, Martha,		P.
1859. Knight, Harriet,		L.
1854. *Knox, Joseph B., }		L.
1858. Knox, Adelaide H., }		P.
1846. Lamberton, Lydia E., wid. of Josephus,	n. r.	L.
1858. Larned, Cynthia E.,		P.
1853. Lawrence, Caroline, w. of Edwin S.,		P.
1862. Lawton, Mary L.,		L.
1858. Lazell, Charles, }	n. r.	L.
1858. Lazell, Harriet, }	n. r.	L.
1855. Levins, Annie McKeon, w. of Maurice,	n. r.	P.
1852. Lewis, Alvin W., }	n. r.	L.
1852. Lewis, Hannah, }	n. r.	L.
1849. Lincoln, Charles A., }		L.
1849. Lincoln, Louenza A., }		L.
1855. Linnell, J. E., }		L.
1855. Linnell, Fanny A., }		L.
1864. Linnell, Mary Frances,		P.

1858. Lovell, John D., ⎫			L.
1858. Lovell, Eleanor, ⎭			L.
1858. Lovell, Edwin H., ⎫			L.
1858. Lovell, Maria L., ⎭			L.
1858. Luther, Emma A.,		*n. r.*	P.
1855. Lyon, Catharine M., w. of J. B.,			P.
1854. Marble, Ann B., w. of Royal T.,			L.
1861. Marshall, George S., ⎫			L.
1861. Marshall, Sophia S., ⎭			L.
1863. Marsh, Clara B , wid of Darius,			L.
1864. Marsh, Emma Frances,			P.
1856. Mason, Joseph W., ⎫			L.
1856. Mason, Nancy F., ⎭			L.
1858. Maynard, Samuel A., ⎫			L.
1858. Maynard, Abigail S., ⎭			L.
1864. Mayo, Harriet Armstrong, w. of Nathan,			L.
1860. McAulder, Mary,			L.
1835 McFarland, Ira, ⎫			P.
1835. McFarland, Judith, ⎭			P.
1842. McFarland, Sarah,			P.
1828. McFarland, Mary R.,			P.
1859. Meade, Harriet, wid. of Edwin,			L.
1855. Merriam, Charles, ⎫			L.
1855. Merriam, Caroline, ⎭			L.
1861 Metcalf, L. A., w. of David,			L.
1864. Metcalf, Margaret A.,			P.
1864. Metcalf, Maria J.,			L.
1861 Metcalf, Charlotte Eliza,			P.
1845. Miles, Jonas M., ⎫		*n. r.*	L.
1845. Miles, Anstis K., ⎭		*n. r.*	L.
1828. Mills, Isaac, ⎫			P.
1828. Mills, Sarah, ⎭			P.
1857. Miner, Joseph E ,		*n. r.*	P.
1854. Mirick, Sabrina, wid. of Elisha,			L.

1842. Moore, Ashley, }		P.
1842. Moore, Lucy, }		P.
1862. Moore, Charles A.,		P.
1831. Moore, Anson,	*n. r.*	P.
1822. Moore, William G., }		P.
1838. Moore, Mary, }		L.
1858. Moore, Mary E.,		P.
1850. Mowry, Losanna, w. of Chas. D.,		L.
1850. Munyan, Mary G., w. of Jonathan,		L.
1858. Nason, Edward S., }	*n. r.*	P.
1858. Nason, Cassandra J., }	*n. r.*	P.
1801. Nelson, Jonathan, }		P.
1810. Nelson, Hannah, }		L.
1835. Nelson, Mary Ann,		P.
1860. Newman, Sarah,		L.
1858. Nichols, Caroline A., w. of S. B.,		P.
1861. Nicholson, Effie,	*n. r.*	P.
1835. Nixon, Harriet, wid. of Nahum,		L.
1853. Noyes, Mary B., w. of Thomas,		L.
1848. Paige, Susan w.,		L.
1842. Paine, Nancy,		L.
1858. Palmer, Mary M., wid. of Samuel L.,		L.
1845. Parker, Alfred, }		L.
1845. Parker, Elizabeth M., }		L.
1859. Parker, Samuel, }		P.
1849. Parker, Thirza B., }		P.
1838. Parkhurst, Harriet,		P.
1841. Perry, Elizabeth Ann, w. of D. H.,		L.
1858. *Phillips, Sidney W., }		P.
1858. Phillips, Addie R., }		P.
1837. Pickford, Elizabeth S., w. of J. K. L,		P.
1850. Pierce, Martha M.,	*n. r.*	L.
1855. Pierce, Lois R., w. of James,		L.

1855. Pierce, Arba,　　　　　　　　　　　　　　　　P.
1856. Pierce, Lydia H., wid. of Josiah G.,　　　　　L.
1860. Pierce, Edwin,　　⎫　　　　　　　　　　　　L.
1859. Pierce, Ellen M.,　⎭　　　　　　　　　　　　L.
1860　Pierce, George M.,　⎫　　　　　　　　　　　L.
1860. Pierce, Harriet N.,　⎭　　　　　　　　　　　L.
1854. Plympton, Lydia E., w. of Alden B.,　　　　　L.
1845. Porter, Samuel A.,　⎫　　　　　　　　　　　L.
1845. Porter, Maria,　　　⎭　　　　　　　　　　　L.
1834. Porter, Susan, wid. of Simeon,　　　　　　　L.
1860. Pratt, Martha, w. of Joseph,　　　　　　　　L.
1842. Prentice, Tabitha L., w. of Henry,　　　　　P.
1845. Putnam, Salmon,　　　⎫　　　　　　　　　　L.
1845. Putnam, Tryphena B.,　⎭　　(1827 P)　　　L.
1848. Putnam, Louisa, w. of Clark,　　　　　　　　L.

1858. Raymond, James,　⎫　　　　　　　　　　　　P.
1843. Raymond, Clara,　⎭　　　　　　　　　　　　L.
1855. Raymore, Elizabeth H., w. of James H ,　　　L.
1833. Read, Abigail, wid. of Samuel T ,　　n. r.　P.
1847. Read, Abby W.,　　　　　　　　　　n. r.　P.
1858. Reed, Jacob,　　⎫　　　　　　　　　　　　　L.
1858. Reed, Hannah.,　⎭　　　　　　　　　　　　L.
1861. Reed, Samuel G.,　　⎫　　　　　　　　　　　L.
1861. Reed, Eliza B. C.,　⎭　　　　　　　　　　　L.
1857. Rice, Catharine, wid. of Asa,　　　　　　　　L.
1842. Rich, Lucretia M., w. of Elkanah,　　　　　P.
1857. Richardson, Charles,　⎫　　　　　　　　　　L.
1857. Richardson, Mary L.,　⎭　　　　　　　　　　L.
1827. Richardson, Lucy, w. of Stephen,　　　　　P.
1842. Richmond, Adeline A., w. of W.,　　　　　　P.
1855. Rider, Harriet, wid. of Joseph,　　　　　　　L.
1855. Rider, Chas. C.,　　　　　　　　　　　　　　L.
1858. Robinson, Sarah M., w. of Johnson,　　　　　P.
1858. Robinson, Susan B., w. of Thomas B.,　　　L.

1851. Rockwood, Fanny P., (1812 p.)   L.
1817. Rockwood, Mary E.,   P.
1832. Rogers, Elizabeth, wid. of Henry,   P.
1858. Rogers, Sarah M., w. of Israel M.,   P.
1864. Ryan, Mary, wid. of John,   L.

1864. Shaw, S. Lambert,   P.
1810. Shepard, Paul,   P.
1864. Shepard, George C.,   L.
1856. Sibley, William,   P.
1856. Sibley, Mary L.,   P.
1861. Smith, Abi, wid. of John A.,   L.
1861. Smith, Chloe B., w. of Moses B.,   L.
1861. Smith, Mary E.,   L.
1861. Smith, Sarah Jane,   L.
1863. Snow, Cynthia,   L.
1858. Spalding, Susan H. T., wid. of Jason C.,   L.
1858. Spalding, Helen T.,   L.
1857. Spaulding, Lorenzo Q ,   P.
1857. Spaulding, Harriet R.,   L.
1857. Spiers, Mary, wid. of John,   L.
1854. Sprague, Laura, w. of Daniel, .   L.
1860. Stockwell, Maria Elizabeth,   P.
1847. Stone, M. D. H., w. of Artemas,   *n. r.*   L.
1850. Stone, Luther,   L.
1850. Stone, Deidamia,   L.
1851. Stone, Sarah M., w. of Phineas T.,   L.
1855. Stone, Maria Louisa,   P.
1858. *Stone, I. Augustus,   P.
1817. Stone, Laura, w. of Uriah,   P.
1858. Stowe, Charlotte C., wid. of Martin,   P.
1854. Stowe, Luther,   L.
1858. Stowe, Mary E.,   P.
1858. Stowe, Alona, wid of Lovell,   P.

1858. Stowe, Emily C., w. of Henry L.,   P.
1858. Stowell, Harriet C.,   P.
1858. Stratton, Harriet A., w. of Fred. A.,   P.
1842. Sturtevant, Abigail P., wid. of Samuel,   L.
1858. Sturtevant, Sarah H., wid of Elisha,   L.
1842. Sutton, Lucy, wid. of Thomas,   P.
1816. Sutton, Mary, wid. of John,   P.
1838. Sutton, M. Rebecca,   P.
1849. Sutton, Emma, w. of George T.,   P.

1858. Taft, Lyman J.,   L.
1858. Taft, Mary A.,   L.
1858. Taft, Helen A ,   n. r.   P.
1838. Tainter, Daniel,   P.
1838. Tainter, Sarah E ,   P.
1863. Tainter, Charles Emory,   P.
1858. Thompson, John A ,   n. r.   P.
1858. Thompson, Eletheah, w. of Prescott A ,   P.
1856. Torrey, Joseph R.,   L.
1856. Torrey, Ann, A.,   L.
1864. Tozier, E. Oscar,   L.
1684. Tozier, Anna B.,   L.
1847. Tufts, Ann B., wid. of Joseph,   n. r.   P.

1850. Wadley, Mary Jane, w. of Joseph,   n. r.   P.
1858. Wadsworth, Benjamin,   L.
1858. Wadsworth, Thankful F.,   L.
1841. Waite, Lydia B. B., wid. of Alvin,   L.
1855. Waite Geo. Alvin,   n. r.   P.
1852. Walcott, Eli,   L.
1852. Walcott, Mary,   L.
1852. Walcott, Edward F.,   L.
1863. Walker, Rev. Edward A.,   L.
1863. Walker, Katharine K. C.,   L.
1853. Walker, Abigail, w. of A. G.,   L.

1846. Ward, Daniel,		P.
1849. Ware, Elizabeth A., w. of A. P.,		L.
1859. Warfield, Stephen T.,		P.
1851. Warren, Dura, }	ꜳ. r.	L.
1851. Warren, Meleatiah, }	n. r.	L.
1855. Waters, Mary Elizabeth,		P.
1855. Watkins, Hannah, wid. of Andrew,		L.
1858. Watkins, Mary Ann, w. of Elbridge G.,		P.
1857. Wedge, Electa S. Nixcon, w. of Richard, n. r.		P.
1853. Wells, Jane E.,		P.
1850. Wheeler, Polly, wid. of Jonas,		L.
1838. Wheeler, Sarah, w. of Erastus W.,		P.
1845. Wheelock, Caroline E.,		L.
1855. Wheelock, Mary W., w. of Eleazer,	ꜳ. r.	P.
1850. Whipple, Franklin, }		L.
1854. Whipple, Eliza W., }		L.
1841. Whipple, Julia L., wid. of George,		L.
1855. Whipple, Nancy, w. of Percival,		L.
1842. White, Leonard, }		P.
1842. White, Emily A., }		P.
1853. White, John C., }		L.
1857. White, Mary L., }		P.
1858. White, Rollin G., }		P.
1858. White, Lusanna T., }		P.
1838. Whittemore, Mary S.,	n. r.	P.
1855. Whittemore, Edward M.,	n. r.	P.
1858. Wight, Charles B., }		P.
1858. Wight, Nancy A., }		P.
1815. Willington, Clarrissa, wid of Clark,		P.
1858. Winn, Eliza, wid. of Francis,		L.
1861. Witherby, Luke B., }		L.
1861. Witherby, Catharine M. W., }		L.
1861. Witherby, George T.,		L.
1864. Witherby, Clara Elizabeth,		P.

4

1858. Wood, Sarah J., w. of Charles,   *n. r.*   P.
1842. Wood, Simeon,   P.
1850. Wood, Asaph G.,   *n. r.*   L.
1858. Wood, Harriet N., w. of Azor B.,   P.
1858. Wood, Pamelia,   L.
1858. Woodbury, Charles L.,   P.
1848. Woodcock, Cynthia, w. of Bela,   L.
1860. Woodward, Joseph L.,   )   L.
1860. Woodward, Julia Ann,   )   L.

1859. Young, Susan, w. of Horace A.,   L.

Present number of members, April 1st, 1864,   575.

A LIST OF
NON-RESIDENT MEMBERS.

With their Places of Residence, so far as known, April 1, 1864.

Alton, James E , }	*Hartford, Conn.*
Alton, Lura J., }	*Hartford, Conn.*
Andrews, John D., }	*S. Boston, Mass.*
Andrews, Rosalia, }	*S. Boston, Mass.*
Bacon, Catharine B., wid. of Samuel,	*Grafton, Mass.*
Barton, Elbridge,	
Blair, Robert Horace, }	*Keokuk, Iowa.*
Blair, Lucy M., }	*Keokuk, Iowa.*
Bliss, Harrietta B., wid. of John H.,	*Nashua, N. H.*
Brigham, Mary, wid. of Hosea,	*Chickopee, Mass.*
Budd, John,	
Burbank, Betsey, w. of Isaac,	
Carpenter, Ephraim W., }	*Cleveland, O.*
Carpenter, Sarah A., }	*Cleveland, O.*
Champney, Francis C.,	
Chase, William M.,	*Boston, Mass.*
Cobleigh, Sophia, w. of Henry,	
Curby, Elizabeth,	*Canada West.*
Curtis, Geo. T. S., }	*Newark N. J.*
Curtis, Harriet F., }	*Newark N. J.*
Curtis, Lydia,	*Brookline, Mass.*
Cutting, Lewis,	*West Boylston, Mass.*
Deland, Hester C.,	*New York City.*
Dickson, Ellen A , w. of Jos. E.,	*Newport, R. I.*

Eldredge, Julius A., }	*Springfield, Mass.*
Eldredge, Catharine, }	*Springfield, Mass.*
Estabrook, Rebecca, wid. of Stillman,	*Quincy, Mass.*
Estey, Emily H., w. of James F.,	*Brattleboro', Vt.*
Fairbanks, Cornelius W.,	*Winchester, N. H.*
Fiske, Matilda H., w. of Walter B.,	*Montreal, Canada.*
Flagg, Jarvis,	
Fuller, Joseph D., }	*Hudson, N. Y.*
Fuller, Caroline W., }	*Hudson, N. Y.*
Gilbert, Mary, wid. of Charles,	*West Brookfield, Mass.*
Gleason, Sarah, wid. of John,	*Charlton, Mass.*
Grout, Emeline C., w. of Jacob B.,	*Stratton, Vt.*
Hall, Fannie E., w. of Alvin E.,	*Springfield, Mass.*
Heard, Nathan,	*Boston, Mass.*
Houghton, Miranda, wid. of Geo. W.,	*Brooklyn, N. Y.*
Howe, Leonard, }	*Near Portland, Me.*
Howe, Nancy, }	*Near Portland, Me.*
Howes, Arlette,	*Ashburnham, Mass.*
Hunt, Ann Maria,	*Marysville, Tenn.*
Kingman, Lydia A., w. of Davis,	*Northboro', Mass.*
Klute, Henry,	
Knapp, Louisa J, w. of Henry,	*Newark, N. J.*
Knapp, Lucinda, w. of Gilbert C.,	*Franklin, Mass.*
Lamberton, Lydia E., wid. of Josephus,	*Ware, Mass.*
Lazell, Charles, }	*Acton, Mass.*
Lazell, Harriet, }	*Acton, Mass.*
Levins, Annie McKeon, w. of Maurice,	*Boston, Mass.*
Lewss, Alvin W., }	*Sterling, Mass.*
Lewis, Hannah, }	*Sterling, Mass.*
Luther, Emma A.,	*Ashland, Mass.*

Miles, Jonas M., ⎫	*Fitchburg, Mass.*
Miles, Anstis K , ⎭	*Fitchburg, Mass.*
Miner Joseph E.,	*Clinton, Mass.*
Moore, Anson,	
Nason, Edward S., ⎫	*Ashland, Mass.*
Nason, Cassandra J., ⎭	*Ashland, Mass.*
Nicholson, Effie,	*Boston, Mass.*
Pierce, Martha M.,	.
Read, Abigail, wid. of Samuel T.,	*Romeo, Mich.*
Read Abby W.,	*Romeo, Mich.*
Stone, M. D. H., w. of Artemas,	*Boston, Mass.*
Taft, Hellen A.,	*Ashland, Mass.*
Thompson, John A.,	*Newbern, N, C.*
Tufts, Ann B., wid. of Joseph,	*Boston, Mass.*
Wadley, Mary Jane, w. of Joseph,	*Munroe, La.*
Waite, Geo. Alvin,	*New York City.*
Warren, Dura, ⎫	*Boston, Mass.*
Warren, Meleatiah, ⎭	*Boston, Mass.*
Wedge, Electa S. Nixon, w. of Richard,	*Amboy, Ill.*
Wheelock, Mary W., w. of Eleazer,	*Leverett, Mass.*
Whittemore, Mary S.,	*Lynchburg, Va.*
Whittemore, Edward M.,	*Hartford, Conn.*
Wood, Asaph G.,	*San Francisco, Cal.*
Wood, Sarah J., w. of Charles,	*Grafton, Mass,*

www.ingramcontent.com/pod-product-compliance
Lightning Source LLC
Chambersburg PA
CBHW021444090426
42739CB00009B/1640